To Dad, With!

Gwen, & David

CARDIFF
A Pictorial History

General view of Cardiff in the 1920s.

CARDIFF
A Pictorial History

Ian N. Soulsby

Phillimore

1989

Published by
PHILLIMORE & CO. LTD.
Shopwyke Hall, Chichester, Sussex

ISBN 0 85033 727 5

Printed and bound in Great Britain by
BIDDLES LTD.
Guildford, Surrey

To my mother,
for all her help and encouragement
over the years

List of Illustrations

Frontispiece : General view of Cardiff in the 1920s

Acknowledgments

It is always encouraging for an author to receive a publisher's commission and I am most grateful to Mr. Noel Osborne of Phillimore for the invitation to compile this volume which quite unexpectedly dropped through my letter box and brightened up a winter's morning. Many of my colleagues have supplied me with interesting source material, particularly Judith Anderson and Brenda Gibbins. To Ashley Hood and Barrie Jones I am grateful for help on the photographic side, while Fiona Banks and her staff cheerfully accommodated me with my many long overdue library volumes for which I should owe a small fortune in fines! I would also like to thank Paul Morgan for allowing me access to his encyclopaedic knowledge of Cardiff City Football Club.

For specific photographs and considerable background information my greatest debt is to John Burke. His familiarity with the various photographic collections pertaining to Cardiff has proved invaluable, as has been the assistance of his former associate Brian Lee of the Cardiff Historic Records Project.

Many of the photographs in this collection come from my own postcard collection and from prints collected for teaching purposes over a number of years. I have tried to establish copyright where possible, and would like to thank the following institutions and individuals:

Cardiff Central Library, 16, 20, 23-25, 41, 42, 51-53, 61-63, 90, 103, 107, 131-4, 138, 139, 142, 157, 159

Cardiff City Council, 32-34, 55, 155

Cardiff Fire Service, 101

Cardiff Royal Infirmary, 113

Joyce and Jim Davidson, 68

David Gilmore, 153

Kevin Murphy, 137

The National Portrait Gallery, London, 109

Tony Rhys Jones and Cardiff Hockey Club, 125

The University of Wales College of Cardiff, 70-72

Brian Warren, 140

The Welsh Folk Museum, 98, 143

The Welsh Industrial & Maritime Museum, 65, 166, 167

The *Western Mail*, 82

Finally, a few explanatory words on source material. I have been astounded by the range of conflicting statistical information quoted in many local history volumes, particularly in the areas of population and export figures from the Bute docks. In attempting to circumvent this problem, I have relied heavily on John Williams, *Digest of Welsh Historical Statistics*, 2 vols., Welsh Office, 1985.

The Growth of Cardiff

Although Cardiff is the capital city of Wales with a population approaching 300,000, easily qualifying as the largest urban centre in the Principality, relatively few of its inhabitants are aware of just how insignificant a place it was before the Victorian age. With its Norman church and impressive medieval castle occupying such dominant central sites, there is a tendency to assume that Cardiff has always occupied a prominent position in the hierarchy of Welsh towns. While this was certainly the case during the medieval period, a visitor to the town two centuries ago would have observed nothing more than a slumbering, if not decaying community of less than two thousand inhabitants nestled in the area below the castle and leading an essentially rural existence. It was the industrial revolution and the rapid development of Glamorgan's iron and coal industries which transformed this sleepy backwater into a thriving port and commercial metropolis.

This is not to say, of course, that Cardiff as a town is a product of the modern age. On the contrary, a small community may have been in existence since the late first century A.D. when the Romans established a fort here and later built a more formidable version on the site of the later castle. As was often the case, these defences were refortified and renovated by the Normans when the area passed into the hands of Robert fitz Hamon and his followers during the 1080s. It was Robert who constructed a motte and bailey castle within the walls of the old fort and there is also evidence to suggest that he was the founder of St Mary's church which was undermined and washed away by the Taff during the course of the 17th century.

The Norman conquest and settlement of South Wales was achieved by their standard dual policy of creating fortified castle boroughs, populated by their own supporters, which had the psychological effect of intimidating the local population while also serving as centres for further expansion and colonisation. In Cardiff's case the small borough was laid out to the south of the castle in the area of St John's church which was also a fitz Hamon foundation. Since this was a frontier community, liable to be attacked by the Welsh, as happened in 1185, it had to be protected by town walls and these are clearly marked on John Speed's map of 1610. The initial defences probably consisted of just an earthen bank, wooden stockade and outer ditch but during the 13th and early 14th centuries, with control now in the hands of the energetic de Clare family, a formidable stone wall was constructed like the one which can still be seen at Tenby.

Medieval Cardiff was probably at its peak during the early years of the 14th century when the population stood at about two thousand. The walled area was no longer capable of accommodating all the inhabitants and beyond the East Gate, the modern Queen Street, the suburb of *Cokkerton* or Crockherbtown had grown up. Still essentially an English town, it was the focal point of a prosperous lordship and the monopolies enshrined in its 12th-century charter ensured its status as the most important commercial centre in the area. Three quays had been constructed on the banks of the river and small trading vessels carried on a busy trade with south-west England, Ireland and the continent. In 1348, however, the town and surrounding area was badly hit by plague. Borough records for the succeeding years show a sharp fall in revenues and this decline was dealt a further blow in 1404 when the borough was attacked and put to flames by the followers of Owain Glyndŵr in what was to be the last Welsh national uprising. By the time John Speed produced his map, substantial areas even within the old walls were uninhabited and in 1801, when the first official census was carried out, Cardiff's population stood at only 1,870, less than it had been 500 years earlier. The town hall was ruinous, the bridge in serious danger of collapse, and the general outlook far from promising.

With the industrialisation of the Glamorganshire valleys came Cardiff's golden opportunity to regain its former status and re-establish itself as the premier commercial centre of South Wales. Its coastal location at the confluence of the rivers Taff, Ely and Rhymney offered obvious natural potential but a direct link would have to be established with the inland iron industry whose growth was in serious danger of being restricted by the absence of an accessible maritime outlet. In this respect, like many other Welsh coastal communities, Cardiff suffered from the handicap that the River Taff was not navigable beyond the estuary wharves. Iron had to brought down the old turnpike road by wagons which could carry a full load of only two tons at a time and transportation was said to be costing the ironmasters £14,000 a year. To escape from this dilemma, it was necessary to look further west, to the Kidwelly, Swansea and Llanelli areas, where a number of small canals had been built during the late 1760s and 1770s. Approaches were consequently made to the Dadford family, engineers with vast experience gained on the West Midland canals, and in 1790 an Act of Parliament was obtained to construct a waterway from Cyfarthfa, near Merthyr, to Cardiff. Four years later, at a cost of £103,600, the Glamorganshire Canal was completed, and by 1812 the Aberdare section had been added, opening up access to the mineral wealth of the Cynon valley. The iron industry responded quickly to these improved facilities; in 1819 the canal carried 42,624 tons, in 1828, 89,839 tons and by the end of the 1840s the annual tonnage had passed the half-million mark, all transported by barges which could carry only 25 tons at a time.

If the early development of the port was linked to the iron trade, the future was to lie with coal. Small amounts had been shipped out for some time, mainly to ports on the English side of the Bristol Channel but, with the new technological advances which made deep mining possible, the potential for expansion was enormous. It was becoming increasingly clear, however, that the port's facilities were unequal to the task. The floating dock at the end of the canal could only accommodate vessels of up to 400 tons and larger ships had to moor on the mud banks outside and be loaded by means of lighters. Colliery owner Thomas Powell had already taken the initiative and established a basin adjacent to the canal for the loading of coal but long delays at low tide still pointed to the economic sense of a deep-water dock. This was not lost on the principal landowner and industrialist of the area, the Marquis of Bute. The association of the Bute family with Cardiff dates from 1766 when John, Earl of Bute and Lord Mountstuart, married Lady Charlotte Jane, daughter of Viscount Windsor, and inherited the Windsor's extensive Glamorganshire estates. The family's contribution to the industrial development of Cardiff now began with the construction of the West Dock, at a cost of about £400,000. This was sited in the marshlands along the east bank of the Taff estuary and a weir was built at Blackweir to supply the dock feeder. The whole venture was a vital step towards linking the South Wales coalfield with the markets of the world. With all the trappings and ceremony of a coronation, the dock was opened on 9 October 1839. The whole town was there to witness the first vessel, the *Manulus*, enter the basin and a holiday was suitably decreed for all. In the following year Cardiff became an independent port, able to register its own vessels. By 1850 coal shipments had risen to over 730,000 tons, boosted by the Admiralty's decision to burn Welsh steam coal because of its smokeless qualities, and the Marquis's determination to make Cardiff 'the Liverpool of Wales' seemed to be no fanciful pipe-dream.

Sustained expansion, however, was dependent on further improving communications with the inland industrial communities. The old Glamorganshire Canal had been a great servant and in 1839 had carried over 107,000 tons of iron. It could only accommodate vessels of 60-65 ft. in length, however, and the sea-lock pound at its Cardiff terminus was incapable of berthing craft over 90 ft. With 51 locks along its 25-mile course it was never an easy waterway to use at the best of times, and like all canals might be closed periodically for repairs and on account of seasonal factors such as ice and, during the high summer, water shortages. With contracts being obtained for the supply of iron rails to Russia, Germany and the United States, it was now clearly inadequate. In 1836 a private Act of Parliament had been obtained for the construction of a single-line railway to connect the ironworks at Dowlais and Merthyr with the port. Five years later, the first sector of the Taff Vale Railway was completed and in 1849 the main line was extended from Merthyr to Dowlais.

The construction of the West Dock and the completion of the rail link transformed Cardiff from a provincial port into an international one. Large foreign vessels could now be accommodated and the industrial world's growing appetite for Welsh steam coal satisfied. By the early 1850s foreign exports were exceeding coastal shipments for the first time; in 1852 no fewer than 887 vessels entered the port, half of them from the continent. In anticipation of sustained growth, work had already begun on the Bute East Dock, destined to be more than twice the size of its predecessor. This was opened in 1855 and four years later was linked by canal to the West Dock. More importantly, it connected with the new Rhymney Railway, also pioneered by the Bute estate, which now provided access to the huge potential of the Monmouthshire (Gwent) valleys. As a result of these developments the port of Cardiff entered a period of unrivalled growth and by 1870 was handling more than three million tons of coal a year compared with less than 166,000 tons in 1840. With the completion of the Roath Basin in 1874 and the Roath Dock in 1887, the figure had exceeded eighteen million tons by the end of the century, despite competition from David Davies' new docks at Barry which opened in 1869. The world's demand for Welsh coal seemed insatiable and the royal opening of yet another improved facility, the Queen Alexandra Dock in July 1907, reflected Cardiff's vote of self-confidence in its status as the 'Coal Metropolis' of the world.

With these dockland developments came marked changes in the physical appearance of the town itself. At the time of the 1801 census, with the population still below two thousand, Cardiff's geographical limits essentially corresponded with those of the medieval borough. To the north, the castle represented the furthest limits of settlement and cattle grazed where the civic buildings now stand in Cathays Park. Across the bridge, on the western side of the Taff, Canton had only about one hundred inhabitants and most of the later suburb remained farmland. Roath, likewise, was just a village while beyond the site of the old South Gate, which stood at the bottom of St Mary Street, lay a few rows of poor cottages where the old medieval suburb of Soudrey had stood, and then an expanse of badly-drained moorland led down to the river estuary. It was only, in fact, in the Crockherbtown area, east of the castle, that any noteworthy changes were taking place – this was because Queen Street formed a part of the increasingly important main road from Gloucester to Swansea. What development there was, however, was modest and when the third official census was conducted in 1821 the population of Cardiff had only risen to

3,521 and it was to be another 20 years before the five-figure barrier was exceeded for the first time.

This initial period of growth was the direct result of the construction of the Glamorganshire Canal and, after 1841, the Taff Vale Railway. Since both features skirted the contours of the old borough and at the same time required the siting of depots and a variety of commercial enterprises close by, space was soon at a premium. To remedy this shortage, the Corporation announced its enterprising intention to make more land available in the southern part of the town by altering the course of the River Taff. This would also solve the problem of periodic flooding which had already been responsible for the undermining and eventual collapse of St Mary's church.

At this time the river turned sharply eastwards at Canton Bridge and flowed across the present Arms Park, down the west side of St Mary Street and on to the Central Railway Station to rejoin the present course just below Penarth Road Bridge. Any change would inevitably make the existing town quays redundant but it was all too evident that the accelerating silting of the river had already made their days numbered. Although the quays had been extended in 1762, even at the highest spring tide there was now little more than 8 ft. of water available and the larger trading vessels queueing up to take on iron and coal were no longer able to make use of it. Accordingly, work began in 1849 to straighten the river's course and by 1853 the 'new cut' had been completed. Once drained, the reclaimed area was gradually developed and Waring's map of 1869 shows Park Street and Wood Street already in existence. Butetown had followed the construction of the docks and new housing was also being laid out to the east in the Adamsdown area, then called Newtown, and along Cowbridge Road East, Bute Street, Penarth Road and City Road. In 1875 the Cardiff Improvement Act was passed to allow the area between Lower Cathedral Road and Wellington Street to be developed and work had also begun on Richmond Road which was quickly to lead to the urbanisation of Roath, Plasnewydd and Cathays. The 1875 Act also enlarged the municipal borough to take in these new communities, the previous limits of the Corporation having been determined in the 1830s.

By the final quarter of the century, then, Cardiff had literally become a boom town and the 1881 census recorded a population of 82,761, eight times its level 40 years earlier. With the expansion of the port had come a host of ancillary trades – shipwrights, sailmakers, chandlers, rivet makers and rope manufacturers. In turn, the prosperous economic climate attracted other employers to the area, notably the Dowlais Iron Works which was built on East Moors in 1891. Such a phenomenal rate of growth, however, was putting immense strain on the borough's facilities. One member of the Hospital Board remarked:

> It seems that no building belonging to any public institution in this town is adequate to its needs for more than ten years or so. The town is like a youth who grows so rapidly that his clothes become too small for him while they are still comparatively new.

Naturally enough, the author of these words was primarily concerned with the increasingly inadequate medical provision and to remedy this a new Cardiff Infirmary, sited in Newport Road, was opened in 1883. Just about every public service and amenity, though, was feeling the strain. New reservoirs had to be built by the Cardiff Waterworks Company at Llanishen and Llandaff to supply the growing population and there was much talk of building a new fire station to replace the increasingly congested Guildhall Place headquarters built in 1853. In that year a new town hall had also been erected in St Mary Street but again there was talk of replacing it with a more grandiose structure in keeping with Cardiff's enhanced status. While that project was to wait until after the turn of the century and the development of Cathays Park, something had to be done to improve the provision of leisure facilities for a community rapidly losing touch with the countryside. The solution was for the remarkably forward-looking Corporation to acquire a substantial area of Roath from the Bute estate and lay out a public park, complete with its artificial lake, which has been a favourite attraction for Cardiffians ever since.

Considerable initiative had also been displayed by the people themselves. Before the River Taff was diverted in the late 1840s the town bridge was situated about 100 yards to the north of the present structure. The natural meander of the river created an area of waste ground near the former *Cardiff Arms Hotel* which the Marquis of Bute handed over to the townsfolk in 1803 for their leisure and recreational pastimes. It was here, 'in the park behind the Cardiff Arms', that the Cardiff Cricket Club began playing in 1848. With the completion of the 'new cut', the size of the Arms Park, as it was already being called, increased significantly and in 1874 Cardiff's first competitive rugby club began to share the site with the cricketers. This was the Glamorgan Football Club which two years later amalgamated with their rivals, the Cardiff Wanderers, to form the Cardiff Football Club, the qualifying term 'Rugby' being a later addition to the name. By the end of the century organised sport in general had taken off throughout the borough. The players of Riverside Cricket Club had planted the seeds of what was eventually to become Cardiff City Football Club while hockey and baseball were also building up a sound following. Cardiff's thirsty sportsmen could also by now enjoy a post-match drink at one of the public houses supplied by the legendary S. A. Brain and Company who had begun operating in 1882.

As Queen Victoria's long reign drew to its close Cardiff was a vibrant, confident community whose growing population continued to exceed all expectations. By 1891 the figure had risen to nearly 130,000, 20 per cent of whom were Welsh-speaking, reflecting the large numbers who had abandoned the poverty of rural Wales in favour of a regular wage packet. Ten years later, exactly a century after the first census had recorded less than 2,000 inhabitants, the total stood at 164,000. Surprisingly, though, this population explosion was not matched by greater political representation. The Great Reform Act of 1832 had allocated one M.P. to Cardiff and its contributory boroughs of Llantrisant and Cowbridge. Many had expected the Third Reform Act of 1884/5 to award at least one extra seat but this was not to be and the anomaly was not corrected until 1918 when the city was divided into three seats, a fourth being added considerably later, in 1974.

As we have already seen, however, such a sustained pace of expansion imposed a heavy strain on Cardiff's ability to provide the required public services. Nowhere was this better appreciated than in the corridors of the town hall in St Mary Street. For several years there had been talk of transferring the administrative heart of the borough to a new site where sufficient office space would be available to respond properly to the increasing range of obligations being imposed on local authorities by central government. After considerable negotiations, the matter was resolved in 1897/8 with the purchase of Cathays Park from the Bute estate for the sum of £161,000. In 1901 the foundations of the new town hall were laid and on the occasion of its completion in 1905 Cardiff was granted city status by the King, the formalities being carried out by the Prince of Wales who also laid the foundation stone of the new University building in Park Place. During the next few years Museum Avenue, King Edward VII Avenue and the Law Courts all took shape and in 1912 the new Glamorgan County Hall was opened and the foundation stone of the National Museum laid. In little more than a decade the new city of Cardiff could proudly boast one of the finest civic centres in Europe.

The decision to create the Cathays Park complex reflected the confident mood of Cardiff and Wales at the height of their international prominence. When King Edward VII opened the Queen Alexandra Dock in 1907 Sir Clifford Cory boasted of Cardiff as 'the seat of the largest trade in the world for the export of coal'. Neither was this claim a piece of exaggerated rhetoric uttered in the excitement of the great day. New trading records seemed to be set every year and by 1913 coal shipments from the Bute Docks amounted to 24,577,000 tons. Added to this were another 15,500,000 tons shipped annually from nearby Barry and Penarth. It would have taken a prophet of biblical proportions to have predicted not just the approaching conflict with Germany and her allies but the cataclysmic slump in the volume of world trade which was to follow the Great War.

Just as 1913 was to represent the peak of Welsh coal exports, the year also marked the pinnacle of Cardiff's maritime fortunes. There was a short-lived artificial boom in 1919 but thereafter world demand for coal declined drastically and by the mid-1920s nearly half of Wales' quarter of a million miners had been laid off. In 1913, 98 per cent of the world's shipping had been coal-fired; by 1930 the figure had fallen below half. In Wales everything had seemed to mirror the price of coal – livestock prices, the marriage rate, even rugby results peaked when demand for Welsh coal was greatest. With its economic well-being so intertwined with the economy of the industrial valleys, Cardiff's fortunes slumped along with the rest of South Wales. The city had never really built up a strong import trade other than in commodities associated with mining and steel, and with demand falling the unemployment queues began to lengthen alarmingly. In 1923 unemployment in Wales averaged 6.4 per cent, in 1925, 16.5 per cent, and three years later, 23 per cent. During the same period the value of trade handled by the port of Cardiff fell from £58,000,000 a year to £21,000,000. Ships of 5,000 tons which had been built at a cost of £175,000 were being sold for £7,000 or less. The City Council did what they could; a booklet was produced to entice new investment, and a film extolling Cardiff's commercial merits was commissioned and shown in over forty cinemas throughout the country. The writing, though, was on the wall. Cardiff had mushroomed because of the industrial world's demand for coal. If a new role could not be found, the community might fall into the same progressive decline as it had experienced during the 15th and 16th centuries.

The Second World War brought a modest upturn in Cardiff's economic fortunes but the indisputable fact remained that oil had superseded coal and the Rhondda did not yield oil. As a world port, Cardiff was finished, but in a sense so had Cardiff finished with its port. Increasing automation had steadily been reducing the number of Cardiffians who were directly employed in the docks even when exports had still been rising. In 1871, for example, 30 per cent of the town's working men had been either dockers or seamen; by 1911 that figure had fallen to 16 per cent. The elevation of the city to the status of capital of Wales in 1956, in the face of strong opposition from Aberystwyth and Caernarfon, was a reflection not of Cardiff's maritime past, but rather of its new role as the administrative, retail, banking and commercial centre of the Principality.

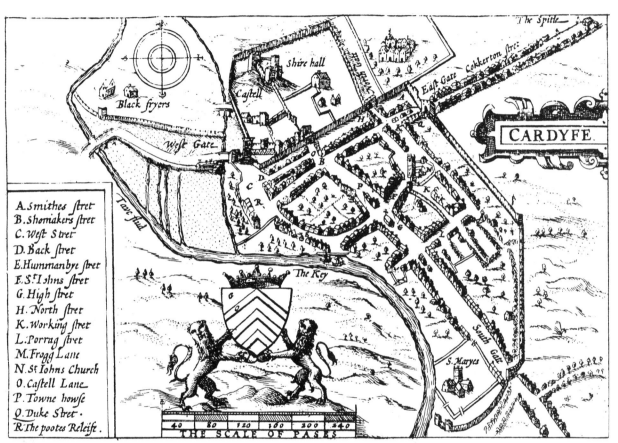

1. John Speed was one of the pioneers of cartography in this country. Queen Elizabeth I was his most prominent patron, and in 1610 he produced his *Theatre of the Empire of Great Britaine* from which this plan of Cardiff is taken. Notice the medieval town walls and gates, and St Mary's church which was washed away by the Taff.

2. This is one of the earliest views of Cardiff, drawn by **F. Place** in 1678. The vantage point is the Canton side of the River Taff which then flowed along Westgate Street. Notice the old town quay and the surviving stretch of the town wall. On the far left stands the tower of St John's church.

3. An early drawing by J. G. Spurgeon of the Norman motte and keep which stands within the grounds of Cardiff Castle. It was built *c.*1080 by Robert fitz Hamon, who described himself as 'Prince of Glamorgan ... Lord of Cardiff ... and near kinsman of the King'.

4.   This is how the busy Kingsway area appeared to Paul Standby in 1775. The castle wall, partly covered by a high bank, is on the right. Notice the old North Gate, sometimes called the Senghenydd Gate, which stood near the modern *Rose and Crown*. It was demolished in 1786.

5.   Compare this view with the previous picture and notice the addition of the Glamorganshire Canal which was opened in 1794. The canal cut under Kingsway and Queen Street, followed the course of the medieval town ditch through the modern St David's Centre, and on to the docks.

6. St John's church is the oldest Cardiff building to be still in constant use. Built in the 12th century, it was originally inferior to St Mary's but, following the mother church's demise at the hands of the River Taff, St John's assumed the mantle of the borough's principal place of worship. The present structure is largely the result of rebuilding in the 15th century.

7. On 12 November 1766, John, Earl of Bute and Lord Mountstuart, married Charlotte, eldest daughter of Herbert, Viscount Windsor, and so inherited the Windsor's extensive lands in and around Cardiff. In 1796 he was created the first Marquis of Bute and Baron Cardiff.

8. Loading coal in Cardiff in 1820. Although the Welsh coal industry was still in its infancy, 84,427 tons were shipped from Cardiff in that year and the sort of facilities shown here were becoming inadequate. In 1828 the Marquis of Bute commissioned a report on the problem and six years later work began on the West Dock.

9.   The old town hall, viewed from the castle ramparts. The first town hall, also in High Street, dates from 1338 and John Speed recorded it on his map of 1610. It was demolished in 1743 and replaced four years later by the structure shown here. This in turn became redundant in 1853 with the completion of a new building in St Mary Street and was pulled down in 1861.

10.   Rowlandson's aquatint of Cardiff Castle, 1799. This is interesting because it shows the clutter of small houses which lined the south wall and opened onto Duke Street. The last of them were not removed until the early 1920s when a length of Roman wall was discovered. This was retained when the south wall was rebuilt and remains clearly visible.

11. This scene reminds us of the old course of the River Taff when it skirted the western side of St Mary Street. There was a small shipyard in the foreground owned by John Batchelor. The *Central Hotel* at the top of Penarth Road now occupies its site.

12. Apart from a small stretch on the Kingsway corner of the castle, hardly anything remains of the formidable stone walls which defended medieval Cardiff. They were virtually intact when Speed drew his town map in 1610 but succumbed to 19th-century expansion. This was one of the last sections to survive, photographed *c.*1890, at the rear of the old Infants School in the Hayes.

13. Joseph Lord's engraving of Llandaff Cathedral, *c*.1715. The original Norman building dates from 1120 but there was considerable enlargement and rebuilding after 1170. Comprehensive restoration work was carried out by John Pritchard between 1843 and 1867 when a west tower was added.

14. Among the oldest of public houses in Cardiff is the *Cow and Snuffers* in Llandaff North, named as a result of a competition to find the most meaningless name possible! The future prime minister, Disraeli, is said to have stayed here while courting the wealthy Mrs. Wyndham Lewis whom he married in 1839. The inn was rebuilt in 1905.

15. The south view of Cardiff Castle as it appeared in the early 1920s, complete with vines which the third Marquis of Bute planted in 1877. Notice the Animal Wall, designed by William Frame of Cardiff, which was moved westwards in 1931 to accommodate road improvements. The castle was granted to the City Corporation by the Bute estate in 1948.

16. During the 1890s the third Marquis of Bute decided to create a passage from the castle to the gardens on the opposite side of North Road. Here we see workmen clearing the bank which had accumulated along the east wall – only to make the exciting discovery of a long stretch of old Roman wall which was duly preserved for posterity.

17. The original bridge across the River Taff stood about 100 yards upstream from today's crossing and linked up with the West Gate adjoining the castle. The West Gate was demolished in 1781 to widen the road and a decision was made to construct a new bridge further south which would lead into Castle Street. The bridge was rebuilt in 1859 and widened in 1877 and 1931.

18. The tower of St John's church dominates this congested scene of the commercial centre, viewed from the castle ramparts. The south-west corner corresponds to the modern Kingsway. Notice the row of buildings which stood in front of the castle and made Duke Street extremely narrow. They were demolished in 1923.

19. Compare this with the previous view and you can see the effects of road widening which had taken place by the early 1920s. The entrance to Queen Street, though, remained very narrow, largely because of the position of the original Evan Roberts department store which was opened in the late 1870s.

20. The widening of Duke Street was followed by clearance work to the south-east corner of the castle. Trees and shrubs were removed and, as can be seen here, the junction with Kingsway and Queen Street was completely transformed. In this busy scene workmen are laying a new road surface and erecting additional street lights.

21. In 1896 Cardiff celebrated its growing importance by staging its own Industrial and Fine Arts Exhibition. The displays, including many models and reconstructions, were laid out on what was soon to become the site of the new city hall. During the six months of its existence, the exhibition was visited by nearly one million people.

22. A tranquil scene in Westgate Street in the mid-1890s. The building on the right, then the Country Club, was the only structure occupying the long stretch leading up to the bridge. Below the Country Club stood the wooden Hippodrome and Circus, opened in 1876.

23. There has been an *Angel* in Cardiff since 1666 when the first inn was built opposite the castle, Castle Street then being known as Angel Street. It served as a coaching inn and by the 1830s coaches were departing for London three times a week, the journey taking all of 15 hours.

24. One of the oldest buildings in Cardiff is the Corner House at the junction of St Mary Street and Church Street. It was originally the town house of the Richards family of Penllyne Castle, near Cowbridge. Although the frontage has changed, much of the original building survives and extensive restoration work was carried out in 1984.

25. In 1858 local architect Peter Price began a campaign to erect a public library in Cardiff. In 1862 the Free Library was opened in the Royal Arcade and two years later it was transferred to the Y.M.C.A. buildings in St Mary Street. Its grandiose successor, shown here, was conceived in 1879 and opened by the mayor, Alfred Thomas, in 1882.

33097. CARDIFF: ST. MARY STREET.

26. St Mary Street from the south as it appeared in 1917. The Bute monument and the *Great Western Hotel* are on the left while above it stands David Morgan's and the entrance to the Morgan Arcade. The street is named after St Mary's church which was undermined by the Taff when the river followed its old course.

27. This was Cardiff's third town hall which was opened in June 1854 by the mayor, John Batchelor. It occupied a site on the west side of St Mary Street where the Commercial Bank of Wales now stands. It became redundant in 1906 with the building of the Cathays Park successor and was demolished eight years later.

28. The statue of timber merchant and boat builder John Batchelor, 'the friend of Freedom', still stands in the Hayes. He moved to Cardiff in 1843 and became mayor in 1853. Batchelor supported a whole range of radical and nonconformist causes and frequently clashed with the Tory Butes, ending up virtually bankrupt. His statue was erected in 1886.

29. John Batchelor's shipyard constructed many fine sailing ships like these, the last being the *Ella Nichol*, launched in 1872. Many brought tea from India and on the return passage carried Welsh coal to Australia and emigrants at £17 a head. It is ironic to think that Australians now export their surplus coal to Wales.

30. John Patrick Crichton-Stuart, third Marquis of Bute, and his mother, Sophia. He was responsible for converting Cardiff Castle into a fine Victorian residence and also commissioned the building of the Clock Tower. He became mayor in 1880 and shortly before his death in 1899 sold Cathays Park to the Corporation for the building of the civic centre complex.

31. Castell Coch, Tongwynlais, is one of the most recognisable landmarks in the Cardiff area. The 'Red Castle' dates from the mid-13th century but it was rebuilt by William Burgess in 1870 as a 'folly' for the third Marquis of Bute. The interior decorations and furnishings are marvellous examples of Victoriana at its most unrestrained.

Edward the seventh by the Grace of God

of the United Kingdom of Great Britain and Ireland and of the British Dominions beyond the Seas King Defender of the Faith **To all to whom** these Presents shall come Greeting Whereas we for divers good causes and considerations Us thereunto moving are graciously pleased to raise the County Borough of Cardiff to the rank of a city and to grant now and for the time to come the title of Lord Mayor to the Chief Magistrate for the time being of the city of Cardiff **Now therefore Know Ye** that we of Our especial Grace and favour and mere motion Do by this Our Royal Charter will ordain constitute declare and appoint that Our said Borough of Cardiff shall henceforth for the future and for ever hereafter be a city and shall be called and styled "The City of Cardiff" instead of the Borough of Cardiff and shall have all such rank liberties privileges and immunities as are incident to a city **And** further know Ye that Our further will and pleasure is and we do hereby declare and ordain that from and after the date of these presents the Chief Magistrate now and for the time being of the said Borough of Cardiff so constituted a city as aforesaid shall be styled entitled and called Lord Mayor of Cardiff **And** we do hereby authorize and empower the said Chief Magistrate now and for the time being henceforth at all times to assume and use and to be called and named by the style title and appellation of Lord Mayor of Cardiff and to enjoy and use all and singular the rights privileges preeminences and advantages to the degree of a lord mayor in all things duly and of right belonging **And** we do further declare and direct that the Mayor Aldermen and Burgesses of Our said Borough of Cardiff shall henceforth and by virtue of this Our Royal Charter be one body politic and corporate by the name and style of "The Lord Mayor Aldermen and Citizens of the City of Cardiff" with all such and the same powers and privileges as they would have had as the Mayor Aldermen and Burgesses of the said Borough and as if they had been incorporated by the name of The Lord Mayor Aldermen and Citizens of the City of Cardiff instead of the Mayor Aldermen and Burgesses of the Borough of Cardiff **In Witness** whereof we have caused these Our letters to be made Patent **Witness** Ourself at Westminster the twenty eighth day of October in the fifth year of Our Reign.

By Warrant under the King's Sign Manual.

Muir Mackenzie.

32.   This is the royal charter, dated 28 October 1905, by which King Edward VII raised 'the County Borough of Cardiff to the rank of a City and to grant now and for all time to come the title of Lord Mayor to the Chief Magistrate'.

33. The Chief Magistrate was knighted at the same time as becoming Lord Mayor.

34.   With the granting of city status it was thought that the new office of Lord Mayor warranted an official residence. The first Mansion House, in The Walk, was originally built as a residence for department store owner James Howell. This is the elegant foyer of its successor built at the bottom of Richmond Road.

35. & 36.   Two views of the City Hall. This was the first building to be completed following the purchase of Cathays Park from the Bute estate in 1897. The foundation stone was laid in 1901 and the building was formally opened by the Marquis of Bute on 29 October 1906.

NEW TOWN HALL & DRUIDICAL STONES, CARDIFF.

37. The Law Courts in King Edward VII Avenue formed part of the initial development of the Cathays Park site. Opened by the Lord Mayor, Alderman R. Hughes, in 1906, they were designed to hold the county assizes as well as serving as the headquarters of the Cardiff Constabulary.

38. The statue of Godfrey Charles Morgan, Viscount Tredegar, in Cathays Park,
erected in 1909. The inscription on the side hidden from the camera records his role in
the Charge of the Light Brigade at Balaclava in the Crimean War. He was M.P. for
Breconshire, 1858-75, and among his gifts to Cardiff was the 17-acre site of Splott Park.

CITY OF CARDIFF CIVIC CENTRE

39. Although few would argue about the magnificence of Cardiff's civic centre, the final result failed to fulfil the architect's original intentions. In this view we see the landscaped raised beds, watercourse and fountains which were intended to grace the area in front of the City Hall. The post-war slump put an end to such a grandiose but costly scheme.

40. This royal occasion was the visit of King George V and Queen Mary on 26 June 1912. The gentleman with the splendid top hat walking between them was the Bishop of Llandaff.

41.   Laying the foundation stone of the National Museum of Wales by King George V on 26 June 1912. Intended 'to tell the World about Wales and the Welsh people about their own fatherland', the museum project was widely seen as confirmation of Welsh national identity.

42.   The building of the National Museum was delayed by the Great War and this official opening ceremony did not take place until 21 April 1927. The King is inspecting the troops while Queen Mary stands on the red carpet talking to the Lord Mayor.

43. When the new Cardiff Infirmary was opened in 1883 the original hospital, shown here, was leased to the recently founded University College of South Wales and Monmouthshire for £400 a year. The college later bought it for £11,000 and the building remained in use until 1966 when it was demolished to make way for a new Engineering Department.

44. The purchase of Cathays Park provided an ideal opportunity to rehouse the University which had outgrown its Newport Road site. The foundation stone was laid by the Prince of Wales on 28 June 1905 and the new college was opened by the Earl of Plymouth on 14 October 1909.

45.   During the summer of 1909 the grounds of Cardiff Castle played host to a mighty Edwardian extravaganza, the National Pageant of Wales. Five thousand participants re-enacted the great events of Welsh history leading up to the Act of Union of 1536. In this scene of unashamed fantasy, Wales lays claim to the crowning of King Arthur in A.D. 510.

46. & 47.   The New Theatre in Park Place was the brainchild of a Mr. Robert Redford and the foundation stone w s laid by his wife on 29 March 1906. The theatre was opened on 10 December and at the inaugural performance Cardiffians were treated to the delights of *Twelfth Night* performed by the celebrated Mr. Beerbohm Tree and His Majesty's Theatre Company.

48. Before the construction of the Bute Docks, the river foreshore housed several of these hoists from which coal was tipped into waiting vessels. Thomas Powell, who opened his first colliery at Aberdare in 1840, was the inspiration behind them but, as this scene suggests, only shallow drafted vessels could make use of them.

49. This later scene, *c*.1860, shows the small sailing craft berthed below the coal hoists. Although foreign shipments from Cardiff had exceeded the coastal trade by this time, vessels like these still carried over 800,000 tons a year to other British ports.

50.   The dominant role of the Bute family in the development of Cardiff is clearly shown in
these two drawings from the *Illustrated London News* of January 1883. The upper scene depicts
the Marquis laying the foundation stone of the new infirmary, the lower shows the
commencement of work on the West Dock.

51.   Crowds in Bute Place celebrate the royal opening of the Queen Alexandra Dock on 13 July 1907. At
the time this was the largest walled dock in the world but a less than enthusiastic third Marquis of Bute had
taken a lot of persuading that it would be a viable project. On the same day the King opened the King
Edward VII Avenue.

52.   Known originally as the Bute Ship Canal, the West Dock was opened on 9 October 1839. It represented a huge investment on the part of the Butes but by 1850 it was handling over 760,000 tons a year, mainly coal. The dock was equipped with 12 coal-hoists as seen in this view of 1920.

53.   With the meteoric expansion of the Welsh coal industry during the late 19th century, Cardiff became one of the United Kingdom's principal timber importers. Tens of thousands of pit props were fashioned on the waterside before being transported inland.

54. The splendid Pierhead building pictured a few years after it was built in 1896. The brainchild of the third Marquis, this Gothic structure was designed by William Frame as offices for the Bute Docks Company. Appropriately enough, it was positioned at the entrance to both the East and West Docks, a monument to 'King Coal' if ever there was one.

55. Five men were killed when this Cardiff tugboat, *Rifleman*, blew up near the Pierhead as a result of a faulty boiler.

56.   Designed by Edwin Seward, the Coal Exchange in Mount Stuart Square was opened on 1 February 1886 by Colonel Hill. Here shipowners, merchants and mine owners traded in coal and huge fortunes were won – and, during the 1920s, lost. Had the 1979 Devolution Referendum been carried, this fine building would today be the home of the Welsh Assembly.

57.   In 1911 the Coal Exchange was refurbished under the direction of the original architect. This photograph shows the re-opening ceremony on 20 February 1912 when almost 1,000 members assembled for the occasion. Notice that the ladies were confined to the balcony. Many of those pictured here were bankrupted by the post-war slump.

58. The years immediately before the Great War saw labour relations at an all time low. There were many bitter industrial disputes such as the 1911 Seamen's Strike. In Cardiff the employers attempted to recruit Chinese labourers as strike breakers and this sparked off ethnic tensions, as depicted in this scene of a vandalised Chinese laundry in Crwys Road.

59. Police officers from all over the country were drafted into Cardiff at the height of the strike. Many had to be accommodated in makeshift lodgings, like these who were housed in the American Roller Rink, Westgate Street.

60. Cardiff coal trimmers come out in sympathy with the strikers. At the height of coal exporting Cardiff had thousands of these 'trimmers' who were responsible for distributing and levelling the coal as it poured into the holds and bunkers. Their pay was 6 shillings (30p) a day.

61. This photograph was taken on 31 July 1911 – delighted Cardiff dockers and seamen make no secret of their pleasure on hearing that the employers had finally agreed to increase wage rates. At Cardiff the strike had lasted for ten days but the new rates were still below those on offer at Newport and Swansea.

62. This photograph of 1891 shows the sea lock at the end of the Glamorganshire Canal and the *Old Sea Lock Hotel* which stood near James Street.

63. This is a fine view of the lower stretch of the Glamorganshire Canal. The *Central Hotel* is on the right and in the distance the docks can just be identified. The photograph was taken in 1912.

64. Despite an unfortunate blemish in the centre, this photograph of the canal is well worth inspection. It shows the south entrance of the canal tunnel beneath Queen Street. Notice the length of chain on the left wall by which the boatmen pulled their way through the tunnel.

65. The paddle steamer *Britannia*, the darling of the Campbell fleet, seen here off Sully Island with a foredeck full of sightseers. The Scottish-based Campbell Line began operating in the Bristol Channel during the late 1860s.

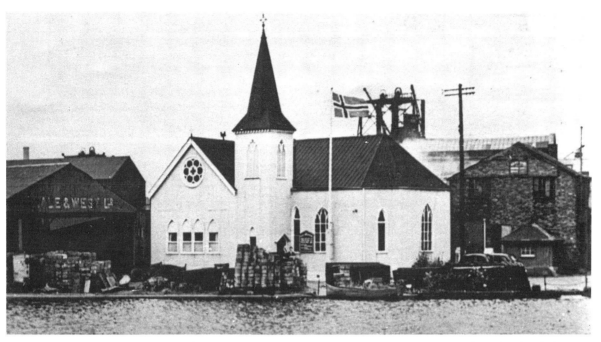

66. With the development of the docks came many strong associations with other countries. Scandinavian timber was widely used in the mines and many foreign mariners set up home in the dockland communities. This is the church, proudly displaying the national flag, built for the local Norwegian community in the docks. Trawler owners Neale and West operated alongside it.

67. The Cardiff Sailors' Home in Stuart Square at the turn of the century.

68. With the collapse of the tin mines in the 1880s, thousands of Cornish people came to work in South Wales. Cardiff accommodated enough for them to form their own society, still in existence. Notice in this role of honour the dominance of the prominent Cory family. Another member, Richard Treseder, founded the horticultural firm which still operates in Cowbridge Road.

69. In 1872 John Cory arrived in Cardiff from Cornwall and founded the family shipping firm. By 1898 the Cory fleet had 23 vessels and exported coal to all parts of the world. This is the Cory Memorial Hall which stood in Station Terrace. Notice the old Y.M.C.A. buildings alongside.

70. Cardiff Technical School in Dumfries Place, pictured in 1898. The institution was attached to the University although it was funded by the Corporation. The School was housed in Dumfries Place from 1894 until 1916 when a new Technical College was opened in Cathays Park.

71. Young men practise their carpentry skills at the Technical School in 1898.

72.   Young ladies at the Cardiff Technical School, Dumfries Place, learning the delights of laundrying in 1898. By the early 1900s the School had over 10,000 part-time students like these and classes were held in nine separate buildings until the Cathays Park college was completed.

STRIKE !
ON THE
Taff Vale Railway.

Men's Headquarters,
Cobourn Street,
Cathays.

There has been a strike on the Taff Vale Railway since Monday last. The Management are using every means to decoy men here who they employ for the purpose of black-legging the men on strike.

Drivers, Firemen, Guards, Brakesmen, and
SIGNALMEN, are all out.

Are you willing to be known as a

Blackleg ?

If you accept employment on the Taff Vale, that is what you will be known by. On arriving at Cardiff, call at the above address, where you can get information and assistance.

RICHARD BELL,
General Secretary.

73. In 1900/1 Cardiff became the centre of interest for the British labour movement. On 20 August 1900 workers employed by the Taff Vale Railway Company went on strike over union recognition. The employers lost considerable revenue and decided to take their case to the courts.

74. The Taff Vale Railway was opened in 1841 and linked Cardiff with the industrial valleys. This is the original entrance to the Queen Street station, pictured before the building of a new station in 1887.

75. The House of Lords ruled that the union, the Amalgamated Society of Railway Servants, could be sued for damages and a figure of £23,000 was agreed upon. This is the cheque for that amount which the union had to find. The legal judgement naturally alarmed all trade unionists and it was overturned by the Trades Disputes Act of 1906.

Amalgamated Society of Railway Servants
OF ENGLAND, IRELAND, SCOTLAND AND WALES.

No. 7036

London, March 18 1903

To the National Provincial Bank of England

BISHOPSGATE STREET CORNER OF THREADNEEDLE STREET, LONDON.

Pay Taff Vale Railway Co. or Order

Twenty three Thousand Pounds

£23,000

Richard Bell   General Secretary.

76. The opening of the Taff Vale Railway did not have an immediate effect on the fortunes of the Glamorganshire Canal and the waterway continued to carry considerable cargoes of coal until well into the 20th century. One of its shortcomings, though, was that it had to be closed periodically to allow for dredging and repairs.

77.   Between 1860 and 1914 a staggering 16,000 Welsh miners lost their lives in colliery accidents. This sorry sight is the funeral of the Jenkins brothers of Dalton Street, Cathays, who died in October 1913 when an explosion at the Universal Colliery, Senghennydd, killed 439 men and boys in what was the worst mining disaster in Welsh history.

78. This is master draper David Morgan, founder of the well-known Cardiff department store. He was born into a Welsh-speaking hill farming family near Builth in 1833. In the 1850s he opened his first shops in Rhymney and Pontlottyn and began trading in Cardiff in 1879. During the late 1890s he was the driving force behind the building of the Morgan Arcade.

79. David Morgan's shop, nos. 23/24 the Hayes, c.1880. The shop was at the lower end of the Hayes and began trading in October 1879. This was no. 23 the Hayes and in the following year David Morgan expanded and took a lease on the adjoining property. By 1882 the shop employed 18 staff and their living quarters were on the first floor.

NAT. TEL. 0640.

WILLIAM McKEE,

Rubber, Waterproof, and Athletic Outfitter.

NAT. TEL. 0640.

Waterproofs

For Driving, Motoring, Cycling, Walking, Riding.
Latest Designs and Shades.
At Lowest Cash Prices.

17/6 to 63/-

Waterproofs

Made to Ladies' and Gents' Measurements from Patterns selected.

AT STOCK PRICES.

Physical Culture

DEVELOPERS,
DUMB-BELLS,
BOXING GLOVES,
FENCING.
CALISTHENIC,
GYMNASTIC, &c., APPLIANCES.

BEST GOODS.   LOWEST PRICES.

Surgical Rubber Goods

WATER BEDS on Hire.	AIR CUSHIONS.
HOT WATER BOTTLES.	KNEE CAPS.
ELASTIC STOCKINGS.	BANDAGES.
ENEMAS.	BED SHEETING.
SHOULDER BRACES. &c.	

LADY ATTENDANT.

Fishing Tackle

Large Stock of
FISHING RODS and TACKLE,
FLIES, CASTS, HOOKS, &c.
WATERPROOF WADERS,
BROGUES, JACKETS,

By Best Makers.

Football

Every Requisite by the Best Makers kept in Stock at Lowest Cash Prices.

Footballs 2 6 to 10 6

Contractors to the
SCHOOLS RUGBY UNION

Cricket

All Requisites for

CRICKET, TENNIS, GOLF, CROQUET, BADMINTON, HOCKEY, &c., by the Best Makers, SUPPLIED.

Special Terms to Clubs.

80.   An advertisement well and truly from another age. In 1906 you could find all this and more in William McKee's store in Queen Street. A top quality overcoat could be purchased for 17s. 6d. (88p)!

81.   Charles Street at the turn of the century, viewed from the south. On the left stands the recently completed St David's cathedral church, built 1884-7 to serve Cardiff's growing Roman Catholic community. Many readers will remember Seccombes department store which can be seen at the junction with Queen Street.

82.   Cardiff's Indoor Market has retained its appeal over the years. The present building, the inspiration of entrepreneur Solly Andrews, was built after a serious fire on 27 June 1885 destroyed much of the original premises. The market was re-opened by the Marchioness of Bute on 8 May 1891.

83. Staff of Cardiff Indoor Market pose for the photographer before setting out on a works outing. In the days before comprehensive public transport, it was usual for employers to provide an annual day out like this.

TELEPHONE : 1619 CARDIFF.

OLD ORIGINAL
ELECTRIC THEATRE,
37 QUEEN STREET.

Proprietors : THE LONDON AND PROVINCIAL ELECTRIC THEATRES, LTD., 29a Charing Cross Road, London, W.C

General Manager .. .. W. REYNOLDS-BENJAMIN.

OPEN DAILY 2 UNTIL 11 P.M.

The original PICTURE THEATRE is still the mos POPULAR ELECTRIC THEATRE IN CARDIFF. UP-TO-DATE PICTURES. All the Latest Topicals are shown here.

THE OLD ORIGINAL ORCHESTRA IS ONE OF ITS SPECIAL FEATURES.

Entire Change of Pictures on Monday and Thursday.

DAINTY TEAS served by DAINTY MAIDS from 3.30 until 5.30.

ADMISSION .. ... 3d., 6d. and 1/-.

84. By the early 1900s the central area of Cardiff boasted nine cinemas, five of them concentrated along Queen Street. This 1912 advertisement is for the Electric Theatre, one of the oldest. The city's first talking picture was shown in the Queen's Cinema, now Menzies, in 1927.

85. Notice the old Empire theatre and cinema in this view of Queen Street. Above the tramcar in the foreground, dental surgeons Templar Mallins invite Cardiffians to sample their 'New Teeth'!

86. For many years Ashton's stall in the Indoor Market has been a compulsive attraction with its colourful displays of fish, poultry and game. This photograph was taken in 1923.

87. & 88.   This is none other than Buffalo Bill Cody who visited Cardiff with his troupe of Wild West entertainers in 1891, 1903 and 1904. The whole entourage was so big, 800 adults and 500 horses, that they had to set up camp in Sophia Gardens.

89. This splendid vehicle, complete with Edward VII look-alike at the wheel, belonged to the Cardiff Dairy Company of Atlas Road, Canton.

90. A group of Breton onion sellers, several sporting their traditional clogs, pictured in Cardiff in 1910. They were a familiar sight in many British towns until the late 1960s. Among the regular 'Johnny Onions' to make the annual trip to Cardiff was Jean-Marie Cueff, who made his final visit in 1977.

91. In 1837 the Glamorganshire and Monmouthshire Infirmary and Dispensary opened in Newport Road. Initially it could only cater for 33 patients but the number of beds was steadily increased until the site could take no more. When a new Infirmary was opened in 1883, this building was leased to the University College of South Wales and Monmouthshire.

92. This is the original operating theatre of the Cardiff Infirmary which opened in 1883. At the time it was the only part of the hospital to be supplied with electricity. Initially there was only one House Surgeon, a Mr. C. J. Watkins, who received £100 p.a. plus board and lodging.

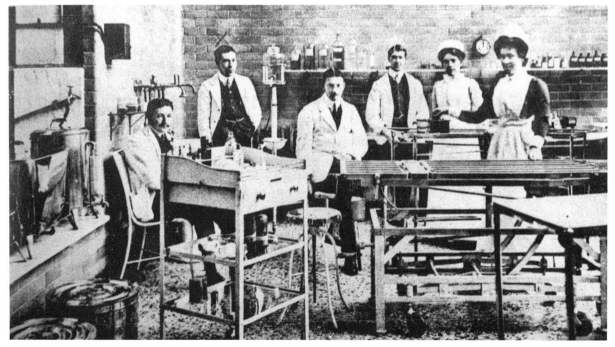

93. This is not a set from an early horror film, but rather the majestically-named Electrical Pavilion which formed part of the Infirmary. The Pavilion was built in 1903 to hold the Roentgen Rays apparatus and Finsen lamps employed in the treatment of tuberculosis, a common complaint of those times.

94. H.M.S. *Hamadryad* was a 46-gun frigate which, in 1866, was converted into a hospital ship by the Cardiff Medical Officer, Dr. Henry Paine, to provide care for sailors visiting the docks. It was moored at a spot called Rat Island and functioned until 1905 when the Royal Hamadryad Hospital for Seamen was opened.

95. A group of *Hamadryad* patients pictured below decks. During its lifetime this floating hospital treated over 170,000 patients. Not all were mariners as it was also used to isolate Cardiff's many cholera victims. The hospital's income came from a levy of 2 shillings (10p) per 100 tons paid by each vessel entering the port.

96.   Before the turn of the century central Cardiff contained many of these squalid courtyards which were mainly inhabited by impoverished Irish immigrants. This was Landore Court in 1891. They were demolished to make way for the expansion of David Morgan's department store.

97.   The *Hamadryad* was not the only ex-warship to find a new role in Cardiff docks. The Admiralty also donated H.M.S. *Havannah* to be used as a 'Ragged School' for the training of young seafarers. It opened in 1866 and was moored near Penarth Road Bridge. By the end of the century it had become a decaying hulk and it was broken up in 1905.

98. This is the old fire station in Westgate Street in 1890. Parish records for St John's church reveal that in 1739 a manual fire engine was kept in the porch of the church tower and that the bell was sounded when fire broke out. After 1839 the fire engines were housed beneath the town hall, moving to the new station in 1853.

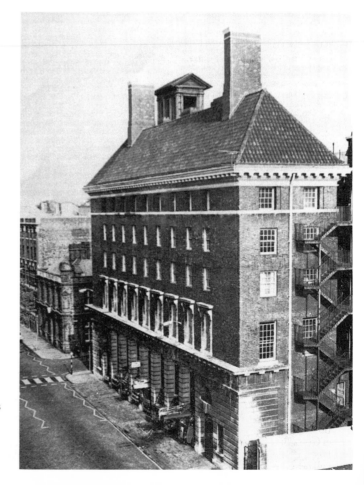

99. The Watch Committee had wanted a new fire station to be sited in Cathays Park but they were overruled by the Corporation. Instead, this Westgate Street headquarters, complete with living accommodation upstairs, was opened in 1917. It remained in use until the present Central Fire Station was opened in 1973 and was then demolished.

100. This is the fire boat, commissioned on 9 November 1912, which operated on the Glamorganshire Canal. It was berthed in the sea lock and was operated by the Cardiff fire brigade. It was constantly manned and had a telephone link with the canal headquarters.

101. With the exception of the Second World War, one of the largest fires in central Cardiff broke out on 20 December 1935. The premises of Cross Brothers were almost destroyed and a large portion of the Central Market roof collapsed.

102. This photograph of
Canton Police Force is
undated but, with so many
officers displaying medals, it
was probably taken just after
the First World War. Judging
by the expression on the face
of the station commander, not
to mention the size of the
sergeant to his right, Canton
revellers were well advised to
remain within the law!

103. The Crimean War of 1854-6, like many of the imperial conflicts of the 19th century, captured the imagination of the British public. Cardiff produced its share of volunteers and here some veterans from the Royal Welch, plus regimental goat, are on parade in Park Place.

104. In 1898, after a long campaign which had seen the death of General Gordon at Khartoum, the revolt in the Sudan was ended by Kitchener's victory at the battle of Omdurman. This is Samuel Vickery, a Canton man who was awarded the Victoria Cross 'for conspicuous bravery' in rescuing a wounded colleague while under heavy fire.

105. The Boer War of 1899-1902 aroused great passions in Wales. Many, like Lloyd George, expressed great sympathy with the Boers in what they saw as their struggle against English imperialism. The general public, however, was soon caught up in the jingoism of the day and here we see Cardiff volunteers triumphantly marching through Queen Street.

106.   Empire Day celebrations at Roath Park School in 1909.

107. Recruiting First World War style. This borrowed corporation tram toured the streets of Cardiff complete with military band on the upper deck.

108. Soldiers and enthusiastic youngsters march past the Bute Monument and the *Great Western Hotel* on their way to the Central Station, *c.*1916.

109.   While the troops were at the front, the nation took comfort in the song 'Keep the home fires burning', written by Ivor Novello. Ivor Novello Davies, to give him his full name, was born in Cowbridge Road in 1893 and had a varied career as a dramatist, actor and, of course, composer.

110. During the First World War everything had to be sacrificed for the cause, even the lawns within the grounds of Cardiff Castle. Every piece of land which could produce vegetables was called into use by Lloyd George.

111. During and immediately after the Great War five Cardiff schools were taken over as temporary military hospitals to accommodate the flood of injured servicemen. Albany Road school was one of them. In this photograph crowds cheer the arrival of the stretcher-borne patients.

112. The wounded display their memento of Kaiser Bill.

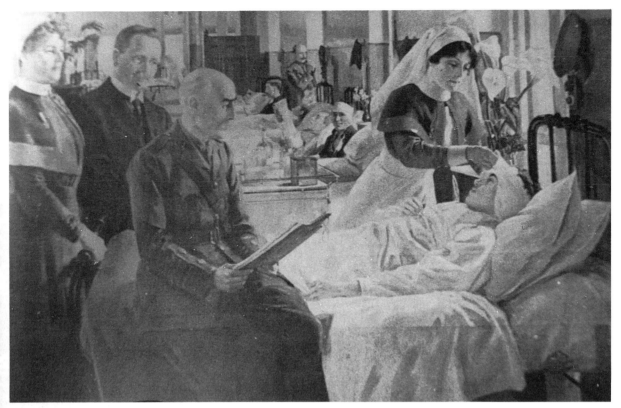

113.   One hundred beds in the Cardiff Royal Infirmary were also set aside for the treatment of injured servicemen. This painting shows Lt.-Col. Hepburn, commanding officer of the 3rd Western General Hospital, and Matron Wilson administering to a wounded soldier.

114.   Whitchurch Hospital, originally the Cardiff City Mental Hospital, was opened in April 1908 at a cost of £350,000. The 120-acre site included the old mansion of Velindre. In 1915 it was handed over to the military and for the next four years functioned as a war hospital.

115. The good ladies of Whitchurch laying on a spread for the convalescing troops.

116. A sea of happy faces throngs St Mary Street on 11 November 1918, the day Germany signed the armistice which ended the First World War. The view is from the castle end with the *Prince of Wales* on the right, partly masked by the tram.

117. Cardiff's memorial to the fallen stands in the centre of the Cathays Park complex. The City Council offered the site immediately on hearing of Germany's surrender. The wreaths shown on this early photograph suggest that it was taken on Armistice Day.

118. This is the *Cardiff Arms Hotel*, the coaching inn which gave its name to the world's most famous rugby ground. Before the building was demolished in 1878 it was used by the players as a changing room. Much of the site is now occupied by the *Angel Hotel*.

119. Organised rugby first appeared in Cardiff when the Glamorgan Football Club was founded. In those days the game was played with a round ball, there might be 20 players a side, and the rules were very different from those of the modern game. This is the first captain, S. Campbell Cory, who also founded the club.

120. In 1876 the Glamorgan Football Club and the Cardiff (Wanderers) Club agreed to amalgamate and form the Cardiff (Rugby) Football Club. The initial colours of black, with a white skull and crossbones, were changed to blue and black stripes after only one season because of parental objections to what were described as 'uncanny emblems'.

121. The Cardiff (Rugby) Football Club side which lost to Newport in the South Wales Challenge Cup on 8 March 1879 at Sophia Gardens. The captain, R. A. Froa, is holding the ball and the gentleman with the bowler hat is the 'umpire', as referees were then called.

122. The first grandstand at the Arms Park was built in 1881 at a cost of £50. It could only accommodate 300 spectators and so it was replaced in 1885. This is a picture of the opening day when Cardiff entertained Liverpool, losing 0-15. Home matches were already attracting crowds of three to four thousand.

123.   No pictorial history of the Welsh capital could be complete without a photograph of
the first Welsh national rugby side, seen here in 1881 before the first ever international
against England at Blackheath on 19 February. England scored five times and inflicted a
rout. Cardiff had four players in the side that day: Phillips, Girling, Mann and Watkins.

124.   Captain Gwyn Nicholls and the Cardiff R.F.C. team, 1898-9. The blue and black strip had become firmly
established, a far cry from the early days when the Cardiff side turned out in their ordinary clothes. On one occasion,
in 1874, a player arrived in evening dress and insisted on playing the whole game wearing his bowler hat!

125.   These splendidly attired Edwardian gentlemen are members of the Cardiff Hockey Club, photographed in 1908. The captain, in the centre of the middle row, was F. B. M. Bulmer while the side also included three members of the Turnbull family.

126. The 1908-9 Cardiff Baseball team. The sport is said to have been first played in the Marl area of Grangetown during the 1880s and by the turn of the century it had become firmly established in the Cardiff area. Its early popularity probably owed much to the large Irish community who were well versed in running ball games of this kind.

127. Cardiff City's F.A. Cup winning team, 1926-7, captained by local hero Fred Keenor (centre, middle row) who made 369 appearances for the club and 31 for Wales. The 'Bluebirds' were born out of the Riverside Cricket Club in 1899, football being something to keep the players fit during the winter. They first began to play league football in 1906.

128. Cardiff boxer Fred Perry, world featherweight and, later, lightweight champion during the late 1920s and early 1930s. The badge on his blazer pocket shows that this photograph was taken in 1928 when the Olympic Games were staged in Amsterdam.

129. Glamorgan County Cricket Club was founded in July 1888 when interested parties were invited to attend a meeting in the *Angel Hotel* by J. T. D. Llywellyn and master brewer Joseph Brain, who had played for Oxford University and Gloucestershire. First class status was awarded in 1921 and this is the 1936 side, captained by Maurice Turnbull (centre, front row).

130.   A packed house at the Arms Park on 20 October 1951 to see Cardiff play the Springboks, the South Africans winning 11-9. Cardiff played the Springboks on six occasions before South Africa was excluded from international competition, winning only once, in January 1907.

131. No sign of the Arms Park in this early view of Westgate Street and beyond. Notice the old Temperance Town area which was developed in the late 1850s. The land was owned by Colonel Wood (hence Wood Street) who sold it to Jacob Scott Mathews with the proviso that no licensed premises were to be built on the site.

132. This is a more detailed view of Temperance Town as it looked during the late 1920s. The various housing acts of the 1930s gave local authorities the power to demolish areas of poor quality housing like these and the 'Town' was cleared just before the Second World War.

133. In 1881 Gladstone's government passed the Welsh Sunday Closing Act in response to the Principality's strong temperance lobby. According to tradition, this prompted an angry John Thomas to throw his newspaper in the air, scream 'anarchy', and sell his brewery to the Brain family. Seasoned drinkers like these were forced to make their own arrangements for imbibing on the Sabbath.

134. In 1910 two general elections were held over the great issue of the day, 'who governs Britain – People or Peers?'. The House of Lords still had the power to overrule the Commons and the Liberal government was determined to end that power of veto. Here a group of Cardiff children re-enact the debate, siding, I suspect, with Asquith and Lloyd George.

135. Staff and students at the wonderfully named Bloggs College, officially the Cardiff School of Commerce, founded in 1907. In the immediate background stand the remains of Herbert House, an Elizabethan mansion built on the Greyfriars site by Sir William Herbert.

136. Adamsdown has consistently been a strong Labour area. This photograph shows local party members and supporters setting off on their annual outing, c.1920. The picture was taken in Moira Terrace.

137. In 1922 the Marconi Company began preparations to set up *2LO*, Britain's first radio or 'wireless' station. The Cardiff headquarters were in Park Place and to establish transmission levels several broadcasting experiments were carried out. Here we see Cardiffian Francis Murphy having his heartbeat transmitted over the air-waves, the signal being successfully picked up in Weston-super-Mare.

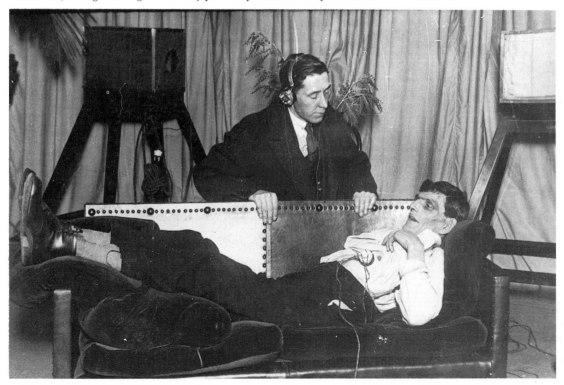

138. & 139.   Maindy Stadium occupies the site of a large clay pit, locally known as Maindy Pool, which supplied the local brick works. During the early 1920s a natural spring was hit which flooded the basin. Local parents feared for the safety of their children, particularly after the death of Lillian Manley in August 1928, and the pool was eventually filled in.

140. This print has obviously suffered with the passing of the years but its rarity warrants its inclusion here. It shows a Summers funeral hearse leaving the family firm's old headquarters in Broadway. The appropriately sombre looking gentleman at the reins was called Ernest Brown.

141. This view of *c*.1920 is of St Peter's Roman Catholic church in Roath, with the entrance to Bedford Street on the far right. The church was built in 1860 along with the schoolroom, shown on the left of the picture.

142. Roath School, *c*.1890, which stood on the south side of Albany Road. Roath still had the character of a village at this time and dame schools such these were common throughout the country. After the 1902 Education Act, however, which placed education in the hands of the local authorities, they died away and this one closed in that year.

143. A fascinating glimpse of the interior of Roath School. The children are writing on slates while one small boy in the front row practises the ancient technique of counting with his fingers. Notice the strap on the lap of the schoolmistress.

144. A rare aerial photograph, taken from a balloon at the turn of the century. This is Deri Farm, Roath, adjoining what is now Waterloo Road. The area was built up during the Edwardian period.

145. St Margaret's church, Roath, in 1865. The author of an 1829 Guide noted that 'the church of this parish is very small', but then so was Roath with only 211 inhabitants. As the area was developed, pressure for a larger church grew and the present building dates from 1870.

146. & 147.   Early views of Roath Park and its artificial lake. This was an area of farmland until it was acquired from the Bute estate for the laying out of a public park. The opening ceremony was performed by the young Earl of Dumfries, son of the Marquis of Bute, on 20 June 1894.

148.   Boating attendants pictured at Roath Park, *c.*1916.

149.   The new Roath Park proved too much of a temptation for local gypsies who soon began to set up camp. They were removed by the Corporation in 1889 but many, like these pictured in the following year, simply moved a short distance to the modern Wedal Road area.

150. St Martin's church, Albany Road, photographed in the 1920s. The foundation stone of the church was laid on 16 December 1899 by the Mayoress, Mrs. S. A. Brain, a member of the brewing family. Her initials are still familiar to Cardiffians, but not for religious reasons!

151. Albany Road was originally called Merthyr Road but was renamed in 1884 in memory of Queen Victoria's youngest son, the Duke of Albany, who had died in France. This photograph was taken just before the First World War. The junior school, opened in 1887, is on the right.

152.   One of Cardiff's earliest taxis photographed outside City Hall.

153. The crew of the Kingsway to Castleton bus pictured in 1920. On one occasion the driver, Fred Deacy of Planet Street, received a commendation from the Chief Constable for overtaking and stopping 'a horse attached to a milk float ... proceeding along Newport Road with no person in attendance' – but for a small boy chasing after it!

154. The *King's Castle* at the junction of King's Road and Cowbridge Road is named after this fine residence. It was demolished in 1892 to make way for redevelopment, including the Davies Memorial Hall.

155.   Cowbridge Road pictured in 1909. The Empire Cinema on the right led into Llandaff Road before that junction was extensively widened.

156. Rumney post office, pictured in 1910, which stood near the site of the old County Cinema. Rumney was still a small village at this time and was not incorporated within the City of Cardiff until 1938.

157. Ely Racecourse, Trelai Park, pictured in 1898. Horse racing was first staged in Ely c.1860. Thousands used to flock to the ground and from 1895 until 1939 when it closed down the Welsh Grand National was held here. The grandstand survived until 1961.

158. Many a racegoer would have contributed to the coffers of the old Ely Brewery which used to be a familiar name in the city.

159. Grangetown is so named because the monks of Margam Abbey were granted land there to develop a grange or farm. The farm complex was rebuilt many times over the centuries and here we see the farmhouse as it was in 1913. It stood near the junction of Stockland Street and Clive Street.

160. Grange Gardens, *c.*1920. Cardiff is fortunate to be so well endowed with parks and leisure areas, thanks mainly to the benefactions of the Butes, Viscount Tredegar and the Thompson family.

161. This tranquil scene is of Fidlas Road, Llanishen, taken just before the Great War. A few years later, in 1922, the parish of Llanishen was incorporated within the Cardiff City boundary.

162. The old Maindy Pool (*see* nos. 138 & 139) became Maindy Stadium after the Second World War. Much of the stone being used in this scene was taken from the embankments of the now redundant Glamorganshire Canal which the City Council had recently purchased.

163. The Llandaff complex of the South Glamorgan Institute of Higher Education in Western Avenue now stands on the site of the old Llandaff Mill, pictured here in 1910.

164. The Cross, Llandaff, in 1905. According to tradition, Baldwin, Archbishop of Canterbury, accompanied by Gerald of Wales, preached here in 1188 in an attempt to recruit men for the Third Crusade. The Cross was restored in 1897.

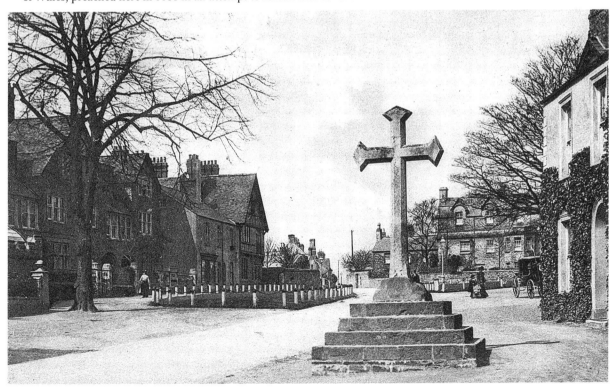

165. Llandaff was incorporated within the city limits in 1922 along with Llanishen, Caerau and Michaelstone-super-Ely. It has managed to retain its separate identity, however, with a semi-rural atmosphere. The village green pictured here in 1930 has hardly changed at all.

166. Ninian Park packed to the hilt on 22 April 1953 to see Cardiff City play a goalless draw with Arsenal. The attendance of 57,893 stands as a record for the club. Ninian Park is named after Cardiff M.P. Ninian Edward Crichton-Stuart who died in action at the Battle of Loos in October 1915.

167.   This collection appropriately ends with this splendid view of the Civic Centre taken in the late 1950s. The idea of building this complex was first mooted in 1858 but interest waned until the late 1880s. Protracted negotiations with the Marquis of Bute were finally completed in 1897 when he agreed to release 57 acres at a cost of £159,523.